Finding Out About
VICTORIAN LONDON

Michael Rawcliffe

Batsford Academic and Educational   *London*

Contents

© Michael Rawcliffe 1985
First published 1985

Typeset by Tek-Art Ltd, Kent
and printed in Great Britain by
R.J. Acford, Chichester, Sussex
for the publishers
Batsford Academic and Educational,
an imprint of B. T. Batsford Ltd,
4 Fitzhardinge Street
London W1H 0AH

ISBN 0 7134 4745 1

Frontispiece:
The pool of London and the City in 1851 (taken from Tallis' Illustrated London in Commemoration of the Great Exhibition of 1851).

Introduction

1897 marked the sixtieth anniversary of Queen Victoria's accession, and Diamond Jubilee celebrations were held throughout the country. During those 60 years many changes had taken place and many of them occurred in the capital.

London had always been the largest city in the country, and between 1837 and 1897 its population had grown from almost two million to five million, with many migrants from both Britain and Europe. Many of them came to the already crowded inner city areas. Their reasons were varied. Many hoped to find work and earn more money; others were fleeing from famine or, like the Jews in the 1890s, from persecution in Eastern Europe. Many settled in already crowded areas where they had friends or relatives, where there was cheap housing and low rents. As with all Londoners, some were able to move to better areas, others could not cope and had to rely on the Poor Law, charity or crime.

An elderly person returning to London after a lengthy absence would have noted many changes. Much rebuilding had taken place, particularly in the City of London, whilst the Thames was now crossed by several bridges, allowing South London to expand. Many of the old slums in Central London had disappeared, destroyed by the cutting of new roads such as Oxford Street and the building of railway stations and lines.

Not that the slums had been eradicated; rather, they had moved out to the East End on to the low-lying areas south of the river. Villages such as Stepney and Hackney now contained road upon road of cheap housing for the working man. Islington, which in 1837 was but a single street, was now part of London, whilst Stratford and West Ham in East London had developed from virtually nothing to have populations of 100,000 and 170,000. In 1837 the countryside was still very near and a person living in the centre of London was only a mile away from fields. But, with twenty miles of new roads being built each year from the 1850s, much of the surrounding countryside was built over.

The first railway in London was the London and Greenwich, opened in 1834, but the horse and the ship were still the main means of transport. Some 1,500 stage coaches a day left London, and the rich had their own post-chaises and carriages. By 1897 London contained several major London termini and an underground railway, and the first petrol-driven cars were being used.

By the end of the century the health of London had improved. Diseases, such as cholera, which had caused thousands of deaths brought home the need for better public health. The Metropolitan Board of Works was formed in 1855 and, gradually, new sewers were built and the various water companies' control ended.

Late Victorian houses in Eltham. Who would have lived in the attics?

Parents were now legally bound to send their children to school, and elementary education was controlled by the London School Board which built many new schools.

In fact, in 1837, London was still very much an eighteenth-century city; public executions, floggings and imprisonment for debt were common. By the end of the century many new buildings, such as the Guildhall, the Albert Hall and Tower Bridge, had been built and many new streets and parks were firmly established. However, many problems such as overcrowding, poverty and unemployment still remained.

This book is about the development of Victorian London. It is not a history of London, but rather an attempt to give an impression of what it was like for people, both rich and poor, to live at various times in Victoria's London.

=Useful Sources=

Much will depend on whether you live in London, or are studying the city from a distance. If you live away from London, you will have to rely on secondary sources: those books written after the events have taken place. However, many of them contain very useful photographs and maps which you will be able to use. The books listed on page 47 will be of use to those of you who do not live in London. The following six sections suggest sources for those of you living in the city.

1. PEOPLE
a) London has its own record office and the Greater London Boroughs have their own local history libraries, many with their own archivist and local history librarian. Make sure that you know what you want to study before you visit and always seek advice from your teacher first.
b) The vicar or warden of the parish church. It is said that London is a collection of villages and there are many parish churches and guild churches in the City. Always check first to see whether the church or chapel is open. Look out for memorials and gravestones which are useful for the study of individuals. Check the age of the church and when any additions or rebuilding took place.
c) Old people. There are very few Victorians still living, but often your own grandparents will have stories which were told to them by their parents or grandparents. There may also be photographs or mementoes in the family.

2. LONDON ITSELF
This is your major source if you live in London. You must walk the area that you wish to study but, if you are seeking a general view, travel into or across London in a London Transport bus; take a map and notebook with you and sit on the front seat upstairs. Alternatively, climb

◁ *A typical late Victorian advertisement which you can find in guides and directories. This one is taken from a pocket map of London.*

o the top of the Monument, or view the city from one of the bridges, such as Tower Bridge, Waterloo or London Bridge. Equally, you might sail to Greenwich from Charing Cross. Learn to identify what is Victorian and imagine what was there before.

3. VISUAL MATERIAL
a) Old photographs. You may be lucky enough to find, or be lent, genuine Victorian photographs, but everyone can consult the collections in the local history library. The photographs are often grouped by area, but sometimes by subject. Collections of photographs are also published (see Books to Use page 47) and often reproductions are sold by local libraries. The Museum of London and the Victoria and Albert Museum have their own bookshops.
b) Maps. So many maps of Victorian London were published, that there is a whole book to describe and list them. They vary from folding pocket maps to large-scale Ordnance Survey maps. You will be able to consult the latter in the library. Ask for the 25 in. – there should be at least two for the period, and they show the shape of houses, and even pillar boxes and large trees. Ask if you may have the section you need photostated.
c) Prints and Paintings. These were the main visual records before the photograph. Remember that they were not always intended to be historically accurate.

4. WRITTEN MATERIAL
a) Documents. These are the working papers of the time and range from bills and accounts to school log books. Sometimes selections are published by the local library, local history society or local education committee.
b) Diaries or memoirs. Ask the library whether they have any written by local people. Many published autobiographies contain references to London, giving details of visits or holidays spent there.
c) Census material. The census dates from 1801, but is only useful from 1841, when a person's age, occupation and county of birth are listed. The census was taken every ten years, and to maintain privacy there is a hundred year rule, which states that no census returns may be made available to the public until 100 years have elapsed. Thus the 1881 is the most recent one available.
d) Local histories. The Victorians tended to write about earlier times, but several contemporary histories have chapters on recent changes. You will certainly be able to use the illustrations, but ask the librarian which are the most sensible to use.
e) Guides and directories. The Victorians were very keen on statistics and detail. Many directories, such as Kelly's *Post Office Directory of London*, were published annually. They list the traders, householders, local officials and buildings and contain many advertisements. You may need to consult county directories for areas which are now part of London, but were then in one of the surrounding counties such as Kent.
f) Newspapers. Local newspapers will be found in the library. Remember that London was often mentioned in the national press as well.
g) Advertisements. You will find these in guides, directories and newspapers.

5. OBJECTS
There are still many Victorian pillar boxes, which can be recognized by the initials V.R. (Victoria Regina), wrought iron railings and pumps, drinking fountains or horse troughs. (Look out for those provided by the Metropolitan Drinking Fountain Association.) As today, tourists bought souvenirs which you may find. Also look out for medals and certificates given by the London School Board for punctuality and attendance.

6. STREET AND INN NAMES
These can give important clues. Camberwell New Road indicates the new road cut in the early nineteenth century, whilst Lordship Lane and Milk Street suggest a more rural past. The Railway Inn or the Bricklayer's Arms may give clues to the date of an inn and the people who met there.

People at Work

The major occupations of London, listed in the 1841 Census, were:

168,701 Domestic Servants
29,780 Dressmakers and Milliners
28,574 Boot and Shoemakers
23,517 Tailors and Breechesmakers
20,417 Commercial Clerks
18,321 Carpenters and Joiners
16,220 Laundry Keepers, Washers, and Manglers
13,103 Private Messengers and Errand Boys
11,507 Painters, Plumbers and Glaziers
9,110 Bakers

Which of these occupations would have been conducted either at home or in small workshops?

LONG HOURS

John Skinn was born in St John Street, Camberwell, in 1837. He was the son of a furniture remover and cabinet maker. In 1923 he wrote his memoir which appears in John Burnett's *Destiny Obscure* (1982).

As my parents were unable to send me to school, I was sent into the workshop to occupy my time . . . . I became useful in assisting my father in many ways. The life in a workshop in those days was very rough. The working hours were very long, from 7 a.m. to 8 p.m. Saturday was the same, no half holidays at that time. The only holidays allowed during the year were Christmas and Boxing days, Easter and Whit Monday (not Good Friday).

How does this compare with hours and holidays today?

From about 1850 the standard of living of the working man began to rise, but the real problem was maintaining regular employment. The building industry was seasonal and many were laid off in bad weather or when trade was bad. However, the growth of London created many new jobs in building, transport and manufacturing and the growth of the City led to an increasing number of clerks.

CO 179

1839]

Collins Joseph, *Boot & Shoemaker*, 11 Old Jewry
Collins Joseph, *Butcher*, 19 Watling street
Collins Joseph, *Tailor*, 3 Albion bldngs. Bartholomew close
Collins Robert, *Coal-merchant*, 15 Swan la. Upper Thames st.
Collins Robt. *Oil & Italian-wareh*. 9 Dorset st. Portman sq.
Collins Samuel, *Butcher*, 21 New street, Covent garden
Collins Samuel, *Ironmonger*, 11 Rathbone place, Oxford st.
Collins Samuel, *Tailor*, 66 Haymarket
Collins Thomas, *Butcher*, 194 Piccadilly
Collins Thomas James, *Grocer*, 8 Leman st. Goodman's fields
Collins Wm. *Bedsacking-maker*, 9 & 17 Helmet row, St. Luke's
Collins Wm. *Glass Enameller to the Queen, & Cut-glass-manufacturer to the Royal Family*, 227 Strand
Collins Wm. *Hatter*, 18 Crown street, Soho
Collins Wm. *Merchant*, 2 Broad street buildings
Collins Wm. *'Plough' P.H.*, 305 Oxford street
Collins Wm. *Skinner & Furrier*, 2 Earl street, Finsbury
Collins Wm. Louis, *White hart-brewery*, Wood st. Westminster
Collinson & Wilkinson, *Who. Stationers*, 83 Upper Thames st.
Collinson George, *Upholsterer*, 28 Store street, Bedford sq.
Collinson Thos. *Tin-plate-worker & Oilman*, 35 Lombard st.
Collinson Thos. Ball, *Gasfitter & Lamp-maker*, 95 Blackman st.
Collinson Thos. Wm. Y. *Tea-dealer*, 7 Crawford st. Portman sq.
Collis Matthew & Wm. *Printers*. 104 Bishopsgate within
Collis Thomas & Co. *Hop-merchants*, 9 Counter st. Borough
Collis Charles, *Hair-dresser*, 22 Lit. Newport st. Long acre
Collis James, *Architect & Surveyor*, 6 Chester terrace, Pimlico
Collis Joseph, *Wholesale Glass-merchant*, 68 Saffron hill
Collis Letitia (Mrs.), *Bookseller & Stationer*, 7 London road
Collis Samuel, *General salesman*, 113 Tottenham court road
Collis William, *Ironmonger*, 11 White lion st. Pentonville
ollison Maria & Co. *Shoe & Patten-makers*, 92 Blackman st.
Collison Francis, *Merchant*, 6 Skinner's place, Sise lane
Collison George, *Solicitor*, 17 Paternoster row
Collison Nicholas Cobb, *Merchant*, 6 Skinner's pl. Sise lane
Colliss Moses A. *Glass-manufy*. 100 Gt. Saffron hill, Hat. gar.
Colliver John, *Smith in general*, 18 Compton st. Clerkenwell
Collmann & Stolterfoht, *Merchants*, 34 Broad street buildings
Collman Horatio, *Surgeon & Accoucheur*, 41 Old Broad st.
Colls & Argent, *Rainbow-tavern*, 15 Fleet street
Colls, Thompson & Harris, *Discount-brokers*, 72 Lombard st.
Collyer & Blackmore, *Surgeons*, 24 Old street road
Collyer Elizh. & Ann, *Booksell*. 5 Prospect pl. Cheynewk. Chelsea
Collyer Clara (Mrs.), *Bootmaker*, 28 St. Martin's ct. St. Mart. la.
Collyer Cornelius, *Window-blind-mak*. 59 Dorset st. Salisb. sq.
Collyer George Samuel, *Army-agent*, 9 Park pl. St. James's
Collyer James Wenden, *Cattle-salesman*, 17 West Smithfield
Collyer James Wenden, *'Cooper's Arms' P.H.*, 19 Budge row

Part of the trades section of Kelly's Directory of London of 1839. How many different trades can you see?

Charles Booth used the findings of the 1881 Census and house-by-house interviews to write *The Life and Labour of The People of London*. The first volume was published in 1889. He described the four poorest groups as follows:

Class A – *The lowest class*, consists of some occasional labourers, street sellers, loafers, and semi criminals, together with the inmates of common lodging houses, and the lowest order of the streets. With these ought to be counted the homeless outcasts who on any given night might find shelter where they can.

Class B – *Casual earnings – very poor.* In East London the largest field for casual labourers is at the Docks .... [They] do not, on the average, get as much as three days work a week.

Class C – *Intermittent earnings:*
— Stevedores and waterside porters may secure only one or two days' work in a week, labourers in the building trade only eight or nine months' work in a year.
— In this class the women usually work or seek for work when the men have none, they do charing [cleaning and scrubbing], or washing, or needlework for very little money ....

Class D – *Small regular earnings.* The men are the better end of the casual dock and waterside labour ... the rest [in this class] are in regular work all the year round at a wage not exceeding 21s. a week, including factory, dock, and warehouse labourers, carmen, messengers, porters, etc.

Why do you think the employers at the Docks preferred to use casual labour?

THE BUDGET OF AN UNSKILLED LABOURER

J. Hollingshead in *Ragged London in 1861* gave the budget of a man earning 18s. a week:

	s.	d.
Bread	4	0
Beer	1	2
Meat and Potatoes	3	6
Butter and Cheese	1	6
Tea and Milk	1	0
Candles and Firewood		6
Coal	1	0
Clothes and Shoes	2	6
Rent	2	0
Soap and Cleaning Materials		10
TOTAL	**18**	**0**

What is missing from this budget? What conditions might make things worse?

This illustration from The Illustrated London News *of ▷ May 1871 shows a family making matchboxes at Bow. They were paid 2½d. per gross (144). The matchboxes were sold for 2/6d. per gross.*

Street People

Thousands of people earned their living on the London streets. The majority sold produce legally bought in the markets or made at home. Others made ends meet by begging, some by stealing. Some had been born to it, others had fallen on hard times.

ICE CREAM

Andrew Tuer in *Old London Street Cries*, published in 1885, described the popularity of ice cream:

> The buyers of the so-called penny ices sold in the London streets during the summer months are charged only a halfpenny; and the numerous vendors, usually Italian, need no cry . . . . For obvious reasons, spoons are not lent. The soft and half frozen delicacy is consumed by the combined aid of tongue and fingers

Why were spoons not lent?

A coster girl from Mayhew's London Life and the London Poor *of 1851. Contrast this with the photograph taken forty years later in Cheapside.*

8

THE COSTER-BOY

Henry Mayhew in *London Labour and the London Poor*, published in 1851, describes a coster-boy:

> The life of a coster-boy is a very hard one. In Summer he will have to be up by four o'clock in the morning, and in Winter he is never in bed after six.

When he has returned from market it is generally his duty to wash the goods, and help dress the barrow. About nine he begins his day's work, shouting whilst his father pushes .... When the coster has regular customers, the vegetables and fish are all sold by twelve o'clock and in many coster families the lad is then packed off with fruit to hawk in the streets.

Why was the coster-monger at the market so early in the morning?

SELLING MILK

Charles Knight, writing in *London: Pictorially Illustrated* published in 1841, described the London milk sellers:

> The cry of "Milk", or the rattle of the milk-pail, will never cease to be heard in our streets. There can be no reservoirs of milk, no pipes through which it flows into the houses. The more extensive the great capital becomes, the more active must be the individual exertion to carry about the article of food ... so that every family in London may be supplied with milk by 8 o'clock every morning at their own doors. Where do the cows abide? They are ... in the suburbs ... in Spring they go out to the Vales of Dulwich and Sydenham. Yet for the rest of the year the cows' grass is carted to their stalls or they devour what the breweries and distilleries cannot extract from the grain harvest.

Knight's account paints rather a rosy picture. What are the health hazards? Why did production of milk in London soon die out?

THE BALLAD SELLER

A.J. Munby, in his diary entry for 19 July 1861, describes his meeting with a ballad seller outside St Pancras Church:

> The trade, he said, was never so good as now: the public concert rooms have created a large demand for popular songs of the day, and the old fashioned ballads sell well too. Has customers of all classes, but mostly young men, shopmen and artisans [skilled workers or craftsmen], who buy comic songs, tradesmen's daughters, who buy sentimental parlour ditties, and servantmaids. These when they first come to London buy the old ballads ... but afterwards they choose rather songs – from English operas and so on – which they hear young missis a playing upstairs.

See if you can find examples of any popular Victorian songs.

The City of London

By the nineteenth century the original "square mile" of the City of London had become the commercial and financial centre of the world. Apart from the city churches, much of the city had been rebuilt by the end of the century.

THE CITY IN 1850

In Murray's *Handbook to London* of 1850, Paul Cunningham shows how most workers in the City lived elsewhere:

> No one thinks of lodging in the City. The great City merchants live at the West-End, or a little way out of town, and leave their counting houses and warehouses to the keeping of their porters; even their clerks, for the most part have surburban cottages. The City, on a Sunday, is a deserted spot.

Why did people who could afford to live elsewhere?

THE CITY POPULATION, 1861-91

J. Salmon, in *Ten Years Growth of the City of London 1881-1891* published in 1891, gave the following figures:

Year	Living in the City	Working in the City
1861	112,063	—
1866	—	170,133
1871	74,897	—
1881	50,652	261,061
1891	37,694	301,384

What two major conclusions can you draw from these figures?

THE RUSH HOUR IN THE 1890S

George Augustus Sala, in *Twice Round the Clock* published in 1859, describes the City at 9 a.m.:

> If the morning be fine, the pavement of the Strand and Fleet Street looks quite radiant with the spruce clerks walking down to their office governmental, financial and commercial . . . every commercial way leads to the Bank of England. And there . . . between the Bank of England itself, the Royal Exchange, the Poultry, Cornhill, and the Globe Insurance Office, [are] the vast train of omnibuses, that have come from the West and have come from the East.

What other forms of transport would have brought workers to the City?

A TRAFFIC CENSUS, 1891

Salmon's book contained a count of those entering the City on 4 May 1891:

5 a.m. to 9 p.m.	1,100,636
9 p.m. to 5 a.m.	85,458
Total 5 a.m. – 5 a.m.	1,186,094
Vehicles entering 5 a.m. – 5 a.m.	
Cabs	18,020
Omnibuses	10,389
Other 4-wheeled vehicles	42,366
Other 2-wheeled vehicles	21,597
Total number of vehicles	92,372

What sort of work would the night workers have done? which vehicles would have carried the most people?

The Royal Exchange, and the Bank of England to the left, in the 1890s and today. Make a list of the changes which have taken place in (a) transport and (b) the buildings.

CHANGES IN THE CITY

John Wilson, author of a *Gazeteer of England and Wales*, published in 1876, wrote:

Reconstruction of buildings in the principal business streets has, for several years, been very extensive. More than half Lombard Street, and large reaches or pieces of many other streets, in 1864-7, were filled with scaffold poles and hoarding. New shops, warehouses, commercial offices, banks, insurance offices, club houses, hotels, and public buildings, are amazingly numerous, and at the same time, exhibit great ambition, remarkable diversities and startling features of style . . . . The passion for ornament, however, is extensive.

Many Victorian buildings still remain. See if you can find examples of the ornate style which Wilson describes.

The Thames

The Thames was a highway, a barrier to be crossed, a great spectacle. But to Charles Dickens, in *Little Dorritt* (1855-7), it was something else:

Through the heart of the town a deadly sewer ebbed and flowed, in the place of a fine fresh river.

THE PORT OF LONDON

By 1851 a quarter of all British shipping was in the Port of London in any one year and some 9,000 foreign ships each year, plus the very extensive British coastal trade. Charles Knight, writing in *The Cyclopaedia of London* in 1851, described the scene:

Nothing is more marvellous in our land than the Port of London. The broad and busy and deep-laden Thames; the noble bridge and its vast traffic; . . . the piers and steamboat traffic, the closely packed and widely extended ranks of coal ships; the trading vessels, . . . the quays and wharfs [landing stages for loading and unloading cargo], the warehouses and granaries, with their millions' worth of produce from every corner of the globe; the docks with their stores of goods and ships, . . . these form, collectively, the grandest commercial picture which our country presents.

Why is Knight's picture so different from that of Dickens? Compare this description with the print of 1851 on the title page.

This print from The Illustrated London News *shows work on the Thames Embankment in 1864 with Blackfriars Bridge in the background. Why was the Embankment built?*

SHIPPING ON THE RIVER

J.C. Platt, writing in 1842 in Knight's *London: Pictorially Illustrated* , described the view from the London Bridge-to-Greenwich steamer. (You can make the same trip today, though the river traffic will be far less.)

> The stranger, especially from an inland county, who takes a passage by one of the steamers which leave London Bridge every quarter of an hour for Greenwich, will be astonished at the apparently interminable forest of masts which extend on both sides of the Channel, where a width of 300 feet should be kept for the purposes of safe navigation, but which the crowd of ships from all quarters of the globe, of colliers [coal boats, usually bringing coal to London from the North East], coasters [a vessel that sails along the coast], steam-boats, and rivercraft, render it difficult for the harbour master to maintain.

Look at the map in the next section and note the docks which one would pass on the journey.

The Thames in the late 1890s, looking towards London Bridge. From where was the photograph taken?

THE DREDGERMAN

Henry Mayhew's *Life and Labour of the London Poor* contains details of an interview with one of the hundred dredgermen found working in the river in 1851:

> To be sure there's holes and furrows at the bottom, I know a good many. I know a furrow off Lime' us Point no wider than the dredge, and I can go there, and when others can't find anything but mud and stones, I can get four or five bushels [a dry measure for grain, fruit, etc.] of coal. You see they lay there; they get in with the set of the tide; and can't get out so easy like. Dredgers don't do so well now as they used to.

Look carefully at the next section and explain why the dredgermen did less well.

13

Docks and Dockers

The major docks were built in the late eighteenth and early nineteenth centuries. Many were surrounded by high walls to prevent pilfering.

A FOREIGN VIEW

Hippolyte Taine, a Frenchman, visited England in 1861 and published his impressions in *Notes on England* in 1872.

> These docks are prodigious, overpowering, there are six of them, each of which is a vast port, and accommodates a multitude of three-masted vessels. There are ships every-where, and ships upon ships in rows, show their heads, and their swelling bosoms, like beautiful fish, under their cuirass [protective copper base of a ship] of copper. One of them has arrived from Australia, and is of 2,500 tons burden.

What cargo do you think the ship from Australia would have carried?

ST KATHERINE'S DOCK

In the *Pictorial Handbook of London*, published in 1854, the author describes the buildings demolished to make way for the recently constructed dock which was opened in 1828:

> The old Hospital of St. Katherine, and 1250 poorly-tenanted houses which stood on the site, were happily removed, together with the vicious and badly-housed inmates, who numbered nearly 12,000 persons.

Where do you think the inhabitants went?

In volume II of *The Land We Live In*, published in the 1850s, the author describes some of the features of St Katherine's Dock:

> These docks are surrounded by loftier walls than those of earlier dates . . . much more completely than those of any of the other [dock] Companies . . . . The warehouses are vast structures, five stories in height, . . . and cargoes are raised into these out of the hold of a ship without the goods being deposited on the quay . . . . Two days suffice for discharging and warehousing a cargo of 500 tons; . . . [previously it took not] less than two or three weeks. A monster crane on one of the quays will lift a weight from thirty to forty tons.

What are the advantages of these new docks?

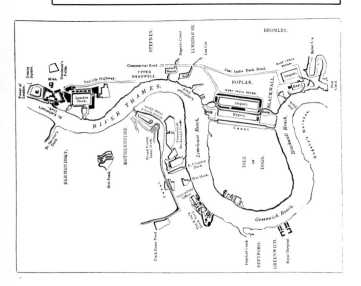

The Port of London in the early 1840s. How many docks are marked?

THE DOCKER

Ben Tillett was one of the leaders in a major dock strike in 1889. He spoke of the problem of the casual labourer to a Select Committee of the House of Commons in 1890:

> Most of the [dock] companies have built sheds and the men get under the sheds in the wet or bad weather which save them from going home . . . the supply is greater than the demand . . . . An average day's work for an ordinary docker is not much more than three hours, taking the year round, but there are times when a gang may be called to work twenty-two hours at a stretch, in the unloading of a mail steamer . . . . To be out of employment is the greatest evil they have to face; to be in it on any terms is a relief.

Why were the dockers sometimes prepared to work for such long hours?

THE DOCK LABOURERS' UNION, 1888

Tillett had earlier been examined by a Select Committee on the 20 November 1888.

> **Chairman: Can you tell us how many members there are in the Society? – About 2400.**
>
> **Does that comprise men working at all the docks in London? – At all the docks and most of the wharves.**
>
> **Are you a dock labourer yourself? – Yes.**
>
> **How long have you been in the trade? Twelve years, I have spent the best part of the twelve years in wharf work, which is identified with dock work, with the exception of the unloading of vessels; all the warehousing is done on the same lines as is done in the docks.**
>
> **How long have you been secretary of the Dock Labourers' Union? – Fifteen months.**
>
> **Is that the only society existing among the dock labourers? – The only bona fide [true] society.**
>
> **How many dock labourers do you estimate are at the docks and wharves in the port of London? – About 100,000.**
>
> **And out of that 100,000 only 2400 belong to your union? – That is all at present.**

Try to find out the outcome of the dock strike of 1889.

Taking on casual dock labour at the West India Docks (Illustrated London News, *February 1886). What were the disadvantages of this system?*

Horse-drawn Transport

CABS

The author of Routledge's *Guide to London*, published in 1871, made the following comment:

> **Travelling in that much abused, but often convenient London vehicle, the cabriolet – or cab, as it is now universally called – is very common. Remember that the fare for one or two persons is sixpence a mile, by day or night to any place within a radius of four miles from Charing Cross, and one shilling [a mile] beyond that distance. A cab cannot be hired from a stand for a less fare than one shilling.**

Why was the fare dearer outside a four-mile radius?

FETCHING A CAB

Molly Hughes, in *A London Child in the 1870s* published in 1934, described the thrill of the cab ride for a child:

> **At seven o'clock in the morning there was no certainty of getting one quickly, and we kept rushing to the window, until someone shouted, 'Here it comes'. . . . They were like the omnibuses with the same dingy blue velvet, only much dirtier, and as they were used for taking people to hospital my father used to call them 'damned fever boxes'. . . . Luggage was piled on the top, and we were packed among rugs, umbrellas, and hand-bags. At last the cabby climbed up to his seat and whipped the horse. It took an hour or more to jog along from Canonbury to Paddington.**

What were the disadvantages of cabs?

Throughout the century the horse was the major means of London transport, though, as you will see, there was a wide variety of vehicles.

PADDINGTON to CHARING-CROSS-STATION—Edgeware-r Oxford and Regent-streets, Charing-cross—every e minutes. 4d.

PECKHAM to GRACECHURCH-STREET—Camberwell-gr Elephant and Castle, Borough, London-bridge—e twenty minutes. 4d. and 6d.

PECKHAM to WEST-END—Some over Blackfriars-bri to the Strand; some over Westminster-bridge to ford-street—every twenty minutes. 4d. and 6d.

PIMLICO to FENCHURCH-STATION—Belgrave-road, P lico (Victoria) station, Piccadilly, Strand, Cheapsi every eight minutes. 3d., 4d.

PIMLICO to the BANK—"Westminster"—Lupus-st Vauxhall Bridge-road, Westminster, Strand—e six minutes. 3d. and 4d.

PIMLICO, VICTORIA-STATION.—Omnibuses to Cam town start about every three or four minutes. frequent to Paddington. 3d. and 4d.

PUTNEY to LONDON-BRIDGE-STATION.—Fulham, Parso green, Walham-green, Brompton, Strand—every e minutes. 3d., 4d. and 6d.

SHOREDITCH-STATION.—Omnibuses continually pas and from the City and West-end, through Bishopsg street. 3d., 4d. and 6d.

SOUTH HACKNEY to BANK. 3d.

SOUTH KENSINGTON MUSEUM.—All the omnibuse KENSINGTON, HAMMERSMITH, BRENTFORD, KEW, R MOND, &c., pass near the northern boundary of Museum and the Horticultural Gardens; while thos BROMPTON and PUTNEY pass near the southern bound

ST. JOHN'S-WOOD to CAMBERWELL-GATE—"Atlas Swiss Cottage, Baker-street, Oxford-street, W minster-bridge—every five minutes. 4d. and 6d.

ST. JOHN'S WOOD to LONDON-BRIDGE-STATION—" Atlas"—Swiss Cottage, Baker-street, Oxford-st Holborn, Bank—every seven minutes. 4d. and 6d

STOKE NEWINGTON to BANK.—Kingsland, Shoredi Bishopsgate-street—every ten minutes.

STRATFORD and Bow to OXFORD-CIRCUS—Bow, Mile- Whitechapel, Aldgate, Bank, St. Paul's, Strand, Reg street, Piccadilly—every ten minutes. 3d., 4d., 6

WATERLOO-STATION.—The "Waterloo," from Cam town to Camberwell, and Old Kent road, pass the tion. Special omnibuses for all the trains. 3d., and 6d.

Omnibus routes listed in Routledge's Guide to London *(1871). The principal routes were north to south and east to west. The first price is for part of the distance and the second for the whole route. On a map of London link up the places listed. Remember that this is only part of the service.*

THE EARLY OMNIBUS

In 1829 George Shillibeer introduced the horse-drawn omnibus. William Besant, in *London in the Nineteenth Century* published in 1909, described the early ones:

> **The first omnibuses were big caravans, holding 22 persons inside and drawn by three horses. . . . They started at nine in the morning, [and] picked up the regular passengers. . . . In the afternoon they left the City at five . . . the omnibus was for the seniors; the boys, when they went into the City at 15, were supposed to walk. When the outside seats were added to the omnibus, the boys began to go into town that way.**

Traffic on London Bridge in the 1890s. How many different types of wheeled transport can you identify?

TRAMWAYS

By the 1870s horse-drawn trams were appearing. Abel Heywood, in his *Two Penny Guide to London* published in the 1880s, described them:

> **These pleasant and convenient means of passage are much appreciated in the Metropolis [city], and when the projected lines are completed, will no doubt tend to thin the number of 'buses that throng through our thorough-fares.**

What were the advantages of trams compared with buses? What effect did trams and buses have upon the growth of London?

London Railways

If you look at a map of London you will see that whilst several railway lines have termini in London, there are very few lines between the major stations. Can you suggest reasons for this? Today we have British Rail, but, when they began, railway companies were privately owned.

LONDON BRIDGE STATION

At first, four companies shared London Bridge Station, which had been opened by the Greenwich Railway in 1834. The station became one of the busiest in London, as Charles Knight described in *The Cyclopaedia of London* (1851):

> There is the enormous Greenwich trade, employing 60 trains a day in each direction. There is the rapidly increasing North Kent traffic, which commanding such stations as Woolwich, Gravesend and Charlton, cannot be otherwise but extensive. There is the South Eastern Railway proper, whose seaside termini now comprise Whitstable, Ramsgate, . . . Dover and Hastings. There is the South Coast which grasps Hastings at one end, Brighton at the centre and Portsmouth at the other end . . . . And lastly the Croydon and Epsom branch which has about 16 stations to accommodate "short traffic" passengers.

Look up the towns mentioned in an atlas and try to decide for which type of passengers the lines catered.

St Pancras Station in c.1868. Note the splendid curved roof. How many tracks are there?

ARRIVALS AT EUSTON

Sir Francis Bond Head, in *The London North Western Railway* published in 1850, described the arrivals platform at Euston Station:

> This platform is infinitely longer than that for the departure trains. It is a curve 900 feet in length, lighted by day from above with plate-glass, and at night by 67 large gas lamps suspended from above, or affixed to the iron pillars that support the metallic network roof. Upon this extensive platform scarcely a human being is now to be seen; nevertheless along its whole length is bounded in the off-side by a line of cabs, intermixed with private carriages of all shapes, gigs, dog-carts, and omnibuses, the latter standing opposite ugly blackfaced boards which are always exclaiming, 'Holborn – Fleet Street – and Cheapside!' 'Oxford Street – Regent Street and Charing Cross!'

Why were there so many different types of vehicle waiting alongside the platform?

LONDON FOG

Henry Leach, in an article "Railway London" published in the 1890s, describes the hazards of fog:

At such big centres of bustle and roar as Cannon Street and Clapham Junction the eye sees beyond the platforms nothing but a network of rails. Here signalmen, pointsmen, engine drivers, all must be ever on the alert, for one little slip might cost dozens of lives. And when the fog fiend asserts himself then must be called the fog-signalmen, who with flag and powder blast do so much in their own particular way to ensure the travellers' safety.

How effective do you think these fog warnings were?

THE METROPOLITAN RAILWAY

The Metropolitan Railway was opened in 1863. Twenty years later, Baedeker's *London and its Environs* of 1885 had the following comment:

These lines, which for the most part run under the houses and streets, by means of tunnels, and partly also through cuttings between high walls, form a complete belt (the inner circle) round the whole of the inner part of London, while various branch lines diverge to the outlying suburbs . . . . [The line] now conveys about 75 million passengers annually . . . at an average rate of 2d. per journey.

Look at the map and see how many main line stations were linked by the Metropolitan Line.

A map of London's railways in 1885. The Metropolitan Line is the continuous dark line.

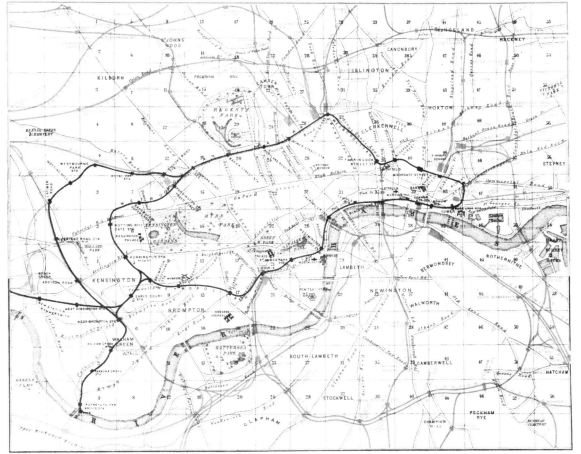

The Slums of London

The rapid growth of London's population made conditions for the poor even worse. Many writers of novels, magazines and newspaper articles tried to draw the attention of the better-off to the plight of the poor.

THE ROOKERY OF ST GILES

Thomas Beames, in *The Rookeries of London* published in 1852, described the old, densely populated streets which were partly demolished when New Oxford Street was cut from Oxford Street to Holborn:

> When the New Oxford Street was building, the recesses [the alleys, courts and narrow lanes] . . . were laid partially open to the public, the débris were exposed to view; the colony, called The Rookery, was like a honeycomb, perforated by a number of courts, and blind alleys, cul de sacs without any outlet other than the entrance.
>
> The streets were narrow, the windows stuffed with rags, or patched with paper, string hung across from house to house, on which clothes were put out to dry; the gutters stagnant, choked up with filth, the pavements strewed with decayed cabbage stalks and other vegetables; the walls of the houses, mouldy, and discoloured, the whitewash peeling off from damp; the walls in parts bulging, in parts receding – the floor covered with a coating of dirt.

Why do you think the word "Rookery" was chosen to describe the slum of St Giles? Do you think it a good choice?

The demolition of Field Lane in 1850. This had been one of the most densely populated slums in London.

WHAT IS TO BE DONE?

Ten years earlier, W. Weir, writing in Charles Knight's *London: Pictorially Illustrated* in 1842, had been concerned about the people of St Giles if the houses were demolished:

> As far as the houses merely are concerned, there can be no objection to this, but what is to become of the inhabitants? . . . Pulling down their old houses about their ears will not provide these miserables with new residences.

The opposing argument was put in *The Times* on 2 March 1861. It questioned why the poor wished to remain in such conditions:

A handbill of the early 1850s was worded as follows:

"CLEANLINESS v. FILTH!"

Do you want a comfortable lodging? Then go to 8, Upper Union Court, opposite St. Andrew's Church, Holborn Hill, where you can be accommodated with a single bed at the low charge of 3d., per night, or 1s. 9d. per week, a good fire and every accommodation. Please to notice, the first lodging house on the left from Holborn Hill.

Gas lamp over the door, Opposite the Public House!!!

Would you have been suspicious if you had read this?

Thomas Beames described a fairly typical lodging house in the same area:

At the bottom of the house is a low narrow cellar, the receptacle of all sorts of refuse; over this, separated only by thin boards, is the common sitting room allotted to the lodgers . . . . The bed chambers . . . are over the common room, and the tenants ascend by a ladder, to a few small rooms where the beds are packed so close, . . .

Why is there no staircase?

◁ *Houses backing on to the south bank of the Thames, c.1860. Imagine the problems at high tide.*

Perhaps it is the attraction of misery to misery and dirt to dirt. Such aggregations cannot be favourable either to public or to private morality. They must tend, not only to harbour, but to generate, dangerous classes . . . . These are the dwellings which they would preserve, and for the preservation of which they would keep Railways out of London. Can anything be more absurd?

Why did Weir argue that demolition made the poor's plight worse, and why did *The Times* argue otherwise?

OVERCROWDING

The problems of the poor improved but the situation was still serious forty years later. Andrew Mearns, in *The Bitter Cry of Outcast London* (1883), described conditions:

Every room in these rotting and reeking tenements houses a family, often two. In one cellar a sanitary inspector reports finding a father, mother, three children and four pigs! In another a missionary found a man ill with smallpox, his wife recovering from her eighth confinement, the children running about half naked and covered with dirt. Here are seven people living in one underground kitchen and a little dead child lying in the same room.

Why did overcrowding make bad conditions worse?

The East End

William Ryan, in an article in George Sims' *London* (1906), describes the scene:

> Take a glance at a small house in a sunless side street. Its customers are overflowing on to the pavement, for not more than half a dozen can stand within . . . . Peering over their heads you catch a glimpse of a room behind the shop. Its shelves are laden with bread . . . . There are two counters. A lad behind one is busy cutting up loaves into small chunks . . . a child whose chin barely reaches the counter wants a farthing worth of sugar, a bareheaded boy of nine or ten with a soiled handkerchief round his throat hands in a plate for a ha'porth of pickled onions.

Why was this shop so popular amongst the poor?

An artist's impression of a Sunday morning in the East End in the 1870s. Why would this scene have such an impact upon those who lived in the middle-class suburbs?

The area east and north of the City grew rapidly. Much of it was low-lying and some of it marshy. The East End housed working people who needed to live near their jobs.

INSIDE THE HOUSE

The following extracts, taken from William Besant's *East London* published in 1901, describe different homes:

> a. **The shipyard foremen and engineers in Stepney**
> Their doorsteps are white, their windows are clean; there are things displayed in the front windows of their houses. Here you will see a big Bible, here a rosewood desk, here a vase of artificial flowers, here a birdcage with foreign birds . . . .

Why did they display things in their windows?

> b. **A docker's family in London Street, Ratcliffe**
> A first floor flat in a house of four rooms and a ruinous garrett [attic] – the street contains 40 houses, each has four rooms.
> There is a table with two chairs; there is a chest of drawers with large glass handles. On the chest a structure of artificial flowers under a glass shade . . . so long as we have our glass shade with its flowers we are in steady work, and beyond the reach of want.
> On the table stands, always ready, a teapot, and beside it a half cut loaf and a plate of margarine, the substitute for butter.

What happened to the glass shade when the docker was out of work?

A WALK THROUGH A WEAVER'S DISTRICT

G. Dodd, writing in Charles Knight's *London Pictorially Illustrated* described Bethnal Green and Mile End New Town. The handloom weavers working at home could not compete with the factories. Their pay was low and there was high unemployment:

> The clack of the looms is heard here and there, but not to a noisy degree. It was rather painful than pleasurable to remark the large number of Benevolent Societies, "Loan Societies", "Burial Societies", etc. whose announcements are posted about the streets; for it is well known that the poor pay ruinous interest ... to societies of this kind. Here and there we met with bills announcing that coals were to be had at 12 pence per cwt. at a certain place during cold weather, and at some of the bakers' shops were announcements that "weavers' tickets are taken here in exchange for bread," ...

Why do you think that the rich preferred to give the weavers food tickets rather than money?

"WORSE THAN PARIS"

The Frenchman Hippolyte Taine, in *Notes on England* (1872), described Shadwell:

> Low houses, poor streets of brick under red-tiled roofs cross each other in every direction, and lead down with a dismal look to the river. Beggars, thieves, harlots ... crowd Shadwell Street.
> ... From the time of leaving the [Thames] Tunnel, street boys abound – bare-footed and dirty.
> ... On the stairs leading to the Thames they swarm, more pale-faced, more deformed, more repulsive than the scum of Paris.

Why did the boys abound in Shadwell and the Thames Tunnel?

East London 1870. View of the Waterlow Buildings erected by the Improved Industrial Dwelling Company. Very soon the old weavers' cottages in the foreground were demolished. (Reproduced by permission of Tower Hamlets Amenities Committee)

The West End

In London the poor never lived far away from the rich, but there were areas where the streets, the shops, the hotels and the theatres were for the rich. This was the West End.

BOND STREET AND REGENT STREET

The author of the *British Metropolis*, published in 1851, described two of London's most prosperous streets:

> **About four in the afternoon, on a fine day, during the season, this being the fashionable shopping locality of the aristocracy, it presents the stranger with some idea of the wealth and luxury of the higher class of the English people.**

PARK LANE

Max Schlesinger, writing in *Saunterings in and about London* in 1853, described the exclusiveness of the streets in which the rich resided:

> **. . . Park-lane, and all the streets around it, are the headquarters of wealth and aristocracy. Plate-glass windows, powdered footmen – melancholy stillness – heavy carriages waiting at small doors – no shops, omnibuses, or carts – . . . such is the character of this part of town, where, among old walls and green squares stand the most splendid houses of the aristocracy.**

What made the area so exclusive?

Westbourne Grove in 1900. Whiteley's Department Store is on the right. How can you tell that this is a shopping area favoured by the rich?

Baedeker's *London and its Environs* of 1885 included the following note:

> **The London season is chiefly comprised with the months of May, June, July, when Parliament is sitting, the aristocracy are at their town residences, the greatest artistes in the world are performing at the opera, and the Royal Academy is open.**

A DIARY OF 1879

Tues. 14 January. Train 10.12 to 0 [Office]. At 5.30 cab to Morton House, dined with Murray and by cab to Ladbroke Gdns. To Musical practice. Danced after. Home 12.20. Liz [his wife] didn't go; her throat not right.

Thurs. 16 January. Train to 0. at 4 to Bucks had hair cut, and get cigarettes and fur gloves at Burlington. At 8.30 to St. Patricks Entertainment, Vestry Hall, Kensington. At 9.55 Liz called for me and on to dance at Hewitts. Very fair but poor music and worse supper. Home by 3. Roads very slippery.

Sat. 18 January. Train 10.12. Very bad day, half melted snow falling. Cab to Piccadilly. Murray came to 0. in morning. Left at 1 with Grainger. Lunch with him and Jones at Club and then to see Panto at Aquarium. In Evng. with Liz to Quartet Evening at the Graingers. Very good.

The diarist writes very little about his work in the City and concentrates on his friends, his wife, Liz, who was an amateur singer, and their musical interests. How can you tell that the writer had an important job in the City and that he was rich?

Houses built for the upper classes in the late nineteenth century.

HOTELS

The British Metropolis in 1851 had a section on hotels suitable for the rich:

> **The Clarendon and Longs are considered first class, and hence are most necessarily expensive. The daily expenses at an English hotel of moderate style are from 6/- to 7/6d. per day, exclusive of dinner, and 1/6. per day for servants . . . . Dinners are to be had at prices varying from 8d. to 10/- each, or more.**

Why do you think the servants were charged less?

London Suburbs

In the early nineteenth century only the wealthy could afford to move out to the outlying villages and travel daily to London by coach or carriage. However, first the omnibus and then the train and the horse-drawn tram enabled more people to live in the suburbs and commute daily. In time, the inner suburbs became crowded and the wealthier groups moved out still further, into the less densely populated areas.

THE CHAOS OF BUILDING

H.G. Wells, writing in *The New Machiavelli* published in 1911, described the rapid changes taking place in Bromley, Kent, in the 1870s:

> **the roads came ... horribly, the houses followed. They seemed to arise in the night. People moved into them as soon as the roofs were on ... already in a year some of these raw houses stood empty again from defaulting tenants with windows broken and woodwork warping and rotting.**

For which groups would you suspect that these houses were built? H.G. Wells was born in 1866. What might be the danger of evidence such as this?

Victorian terraced housing in Tooting for the new middle classes. How can you tell that the area was developed at the same time?

PENGE

James Thorne, in *The Handbook to the Environs of London* published in 1876, described Penge which is between Bromley and Croydon. Fifty years previously Penge had been only a common with very few houses. Then came the railway and:

> **the plague of building lighted upon it, now Penge is a town in size and population ... in appearance a waste of modern tenements, mean, monotonous and wearisome. It has three churches, many chapels, schools, taverns, inns, offices of all sorts, shops, four or five railway stations, and whatever may be looked for in a new suburban railway town.**

Why do you think Thorne and Wells were so resentful of what had taken place?

◁ *The outer suburbs. Note the older Victorian housing on the top road and the late Victorian detached houses below. Which groups would have lived in these houses?*

GOING TO WORK

The majority of working people in a suburb leave it each day for work. Percy Fitzgerald, in *London: City Suburbs* published in 1893, described the daily scene:

> **Of a morning at Anerley, and other stations are seen crowds of busy men hurrying up to town for the day's work. For this the fine air is recuperative; their houses are built in substantial and sometimes elegant style, and overgrown by luxuriant ivy . . . .**

Why do people move out to suburbs to live?

PROBLEMS FOR THE SUBURB

By the end of the century cheap returns for workmen, the growth of the tramways and higher wages enabled more people to move out of London. *The Building News* commented in 1890:

> **We find suburbs, once delightful retreats for the busy city man, . . . fast losing their fair home and reputation. Putney, Fulham, Richmond, Kew in the West, Hampstead, Highgate, Hornsey, Finsbury in the North; Clapham, Brixton, Dulwich in the South, are already being irretrievably spoiled . . . while every acre of land is allowed to be crowded with 50 to 60 houses . . . the higher class suburbs being brought down to the levels of the poorer districts . . .**

Look at a map of London and identify the districts named.

LEE – IN KENT

Thorne wrote more approvingly of Lee, six miles from London and close to two railway stations:

> **. . . a favourite place of residence with city merchants and men of business, for whose accommodation every available piece of ground has been appropriated. Parks (Lee Park, Manor Park, Dacre Park, Belmont Park, Grove Park, etc.) in which houses are not too densely packed, mingled with the terraces of detached and semi-detached villas and genteel cottages, and a sprinkling of older houses in good sized grounds.**

Why does Thorne like Lee?

Kelly's *Directory of Kent* of 1870 referred to Lee's two churches:

> *Christ church* **in Lee Park, is a very neat structure, in the Gothic style, holding nearly a 1000 persons. The register dates from 1854.**
> *Holy Trinity*, **High Road, is a handsome building, capable of accommodating 1000 persons. The register dates from 1864.**

When was your church built? Churches, or additions to them, are often clues to the age and expansion of an area.

The Great Exhibition

Nothing better illustrates the industry and wealth of mid-Victorian England than the Great Exhibition, which was held in Hyde Park in 1851. The Exhibition was such a success that it was re-created on a permanent site in Sydenham, South London and opened in 1854. It became known as the Crystal Palace.

THE GREAT EXHIBITION

William Thackeray wrote the following poem to commemorate the opening of the Exhibition:

As though 'twere by a wizard's rod
A blazing arch of lucid glass
Leaps like a fountain from the grass,
To meet the sun.
A quiet green, but few days since;
With cattle browsing in the shade,
And lo! long lines of bright arcade
In order raised;
A palace as for a fairly prince,
A rare pavilion, such as man.
Saw never since mankind began,
And built and glazed.

Try to find out what part Joseph Paxton and Prince Albert played in the building and the organization of the Exhibition.

The transept of the Great Exhibition, 1851. Why could a building such as this not have been built a hundred years before?

THE EXHIBITS

The Great Exhibition of the Industry of all Nations was divided into four divisions – raw materials, machinery, manufacturing and the plastic arts – and £20,000 was set aside for prizes. The author of *The British Metropolis*, published in 1851, wrote:

> **The department of machinery is the most extensive. Here there are carriages of every description, a magnificent locomotive being one of them .... Every class of agricultural implement has its representative, and there are many of those ingenious contrivances for abridging human labour .... Manufactured machine tools, civil engineering, architecture and building contrivances abound, and more.**

There followed a description of the manufactures:

THE MOVE TO SYDENHAM

The author of *London: Pictorially Illustrated*, writing in the 1870s, described the building

> **The material of which this building is constructed was obtained to a large extent from the [former] buildings. Sir J. Paxton, the architect of the Great Exhibition, was also the architect of the Crystal Palace, and superintended its creation in the years 1853-54. The cost was about £1.5m. The framework of the Palace is almost entirely composed of iron; and the filling in of the frame-work is composed entirely of glass.**

Manufactures are abundant. Here there are scarcely a class omitted, from the rich tapestries, and silks and carpets of France, down to the sewing cotton of Manchester. Cottons, woollens, silk and velvet fabrics, are there in great numbers; unused fabrics, including shawls; those that are made wholly or partly of leather or pile; the paper, printing and book binding; woven, felted, and laid fabrics; tapestry, carpets, floorcloths, lace and embroidery, works in the precious metals, jewellery, etc; glass, china, earthenware, furniture, upholstery, and paperhangings, papier mâché and japonned goods, with a variety of miscellaneous manufactures, will be found in this class. Many of them are extremely beautiful.

Why do you think these two sections would have been so popular?

A VISIT TO THE CRYSTAL PALACE

A.J. Munby noted in his diary for Saturday, 19 July 1861:

> I went down, by a train, crowded with gaily drest people to the Crystal Palace to see the Dramatic Fête, which is now annually held there. The building was crowded, it being a half a crown day . . . .
>
> After dinner – a very bad one – in the Palace, I walked down the crowded lane and went up to the gallery of the Central transept. Flags and streamers of all colours – remains of the Rifle Festival of Monday – were hung aloft . . . troops of brightly clad people were walking to and fro, while the great Handel organ opposite fills the air.

Why do you think that the Crystal Palace was such a success with the public? Try to find out what eventually happened to the building in 1936.

The Crystal Palace at Sydenham. The gardens are now being restored.

Celebrations

London saw many processions during Victoria's long reign. Her coronation and her marriage to Prince Albert were both celebrated. Can you think of any other occasions which would have been celebrated?

THE LORD MAYOR'S SHOW

Max Schlesinger, writing in *Saunterings in and about London* published in 1853, described the procession:

Every year the Lord Mayor elect enters upon the functions of his office in the month of November. The City crowns its kind with medieval ceremonies. The shops are shut at an early hour and many do not open at all; for masters and servants must see the "show". For many hours the City is closed against all vehicles; flags and streamers are hung out from the houses; the pavement is covered with gravel; holiday faces everywhere; amiable street boys at every corner bearing flags; brass bands and confusion and endless cheers! Such is the grave, demure and busy City on that remarkable day.

The Diamond Jubilee Celebrations of 1897. Queen Victoria has been attending a ceremony in St Paul's. Note the massed choirs in white.

The Lord Mayor's procession is still held. Try to find out who holds the position of Lord Mayor this year.

A.J. Munby describes the arrangements for the arrival of the Princess for her marriage to Edward, Prince of Wales, on 7 March 1863:

Sunday 1 March – The streets were unusually crowded, with people who had evidently come out to see the preparations for next Saturday. I hear of shop windows let for that day at 22 guineas each, and of men at Windsor, who have let their houses – opposite the castle – for the four days, for £150 . . . .

Tuesday 3 March – All the way from London Bridge and probably from the Bricklayers' Arms, to Paddington, every house has its balcony or red baize seats, wedding favours fill the shops, and flags of all sizes . . . . In Pall Mall this evening, rows of workmen were supping on the pavement, ready to begin again by gaslight, with their work . . . . While the rest of the population spend their time watching them.

Why were the workmen working at night?

THE DIAMOND JUBILEE, 1897

In *Sixty Years a Queen*, published in 1897, Herbert Maxwell described the decorations:

In the Strand the omnibuses ran under the swaying lines of many-coloured globes hanging around the roadway from one flower-bedecked Venetian mast to another. Round the pillars of the Mansion House and the Royal Exchange were serpentine trails of tiny gas jets winding far up under the dark eaves of the roof and from Buckingham Palace to St. Paul's vast buildings were literally outlined with tiny gas and electric light bulbs . . . many of the houses along the route of the procession were covered with decorations from cellar to attic. The colours generally chosen were red . . . . Draperies of brilliant hues were hung from almost every window, so that some of the streets resembled theatres rather than the busy thoroughfares of a busy city.

The *Daily Mail* of 23 June 1897 described the procession:

The advancing pageant shifted and loosened and came up in open order . . . . Here riding three and three came a Kaleidoscope of dazzling horsemen – equerries and aides de camp [officers attending a king or queen] and attachés [junior members of an embassy staff], ambassadors and Princes, all the pomp of all the nations of the earth . . . . Already the carriages were rolling up full of the Queen's kindred, full of her children and children's children . . . . But we hardly looked at them. Down there through an avalanche of eager faces, through a storm of waving hand-kerchieves, through roaring volleys and cheers, there was approaching a carriage drawn by eight cream coloured horses . . . .

How would you finish this report?

Try to find out how the Diamond Jubilee was celebrated in your own part of the country if you do not live in London.

Public Health

THE LAND OF DEATH – NEWINGTON IN 1849

In 1800 Newington had been a pleasant area south of the Thames. Soon cheap, densely packed houses were built on the fields and gardens. Thomas Miller, in *Pictorial Sketches of London* published in 1849, described an epidemic:

> **... The pestilence stalked like a Destroying Angel. In some houses all died, and after the delapidated building had been closed a few days, other tenants took possession and in two or three of these changes the new tenants also perished – the mercenary landlords never breathing a word about what had befallen the others. The putrid cesspool [a pool or pit for collecting rubbish or household sewage] and stagnant sewer still yawned, and bubbled and steamed in the sunshine, and poisoned all those who inhaled the deadly gases.**

At the time it was believed that disease was spread in the air by smell.

NEW HOUSES IN BETHNAL GREEN

Hector Gavin, in *Sanatary Ramblings* published in 1848, described the once rural village:

> **I found that all the space enclosed between a hoarding on either side of the East Counties Railway, a distance of about 230 feet, [contained] a row of 22 new houses and two flats with cesspools in front, are being built parallel to, and within ten feet. A ditch has been dug on either side of the railway to prevent the foundations of the [railway] arches being endangered.**

All Victorian cities had problems of public health. Being the largest, London had some of the worst. In 1837 there were no health laws for London and, except when disease struck, there was little concern. The 170 separate Parishes found it increasingly difficult to cope.

FOG

In 1888 an poem in *Punch* described a London fog:

> **The King Fog at once descended with the demon who attended his intolerable court, upon the Town;**
>
> **And the day at once grew dimmer, and the sun ceased e'en to shimmer, and the gas-jets seemed to glimmer and die down.**
>
> **All tints save black were banished, and the very roadways banished You couldn't see the lamps not e'en their posts; Faded house and tower, and steeple, and, as for the poor people, they prowled about like damp and dismal ghosts; ... you couldn't see your hand before your face.**

What were the causes of the London fog?

> **The double privies attached to the new houses on the south side are constructed so that the night soil shall drain into it ....**

What are the dangers to health described in these two extracts?

SMOKE

Sir John Simon did much to publicize London's health problems. In the *City Medical Report* for 1850 he wrote:

> Soon after daybreak, the great factory shafts besides the river begin to discharge immense volumes of smoke; . . . the sky is overcast with a dingy veil; the house chimneys presently add their contributions, and by 10 o'clock, as one approaches London from any hill in the suburbs, one may observe the total result of this gigantic nuisance hanging over the City like a pall.

What laws have been introduced to prevent this smoke pollution?

A narrow lane in Lambeth in the 1860s. How can you tell that the lane is close to the river? What hazards might this have brought at certain times of the year? What major improvement is shown in the photograph?

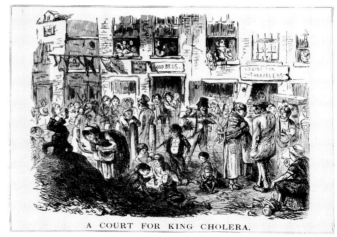

A COURT FOR KING CHOLERA.

A Victorian slum. What evidence is there to bear out the title of the drawing?

COWSHEDS IN WESTMINSTER

In 1847 the Honourable Frederick Byng published a pamphlet on the dangers to health in the Parish of St James's, Westminster:

> There are in the parish, – 14 cow-sheds, 2 slaughter houses, 3 boiling houses, 7 bone stores, 1 zincing establishment.
> Two of these sheds are . . . within yards of the back of the houses . . . . 40 cows are kept in them, each live in seven feet of space. There is no ventilation . . . . Besides the animals there is, at one end, a large tank for grains, a store place for turnips and hay, and between them a receptacle into which the liquid manure drains and the solid is heaped.

From the extracts here, list the major dangers to health in London. You may wish to use some of the earlier sections of the book too. By the end of the century conditions had improved. In 1855 the Metropolitan Board of Works was established to deal with sewerage in London. In time, it broadened its work and various acts of Parliament also helped.

Crime in London

Although punishments were very severe, the level of crime was very high, particularly in the poor, densely populated areas.

THE REASONS FOR CRIME

In *The Bitter Cry of Outcast London*, published in 1883, Andrew Mearns sought to publicize the plight of the poor:

> The lodging houses . . . are often the resort of thieves and vagabonds of the lowest types, and some are kept by the receivers of stolen goods . . . . That people condemned to exist under such conditions take to drink and fall into sin is surely a matter for little surprise. . . . one of the saddest results of overcrowding is the inevitable association with criminals . . . and continual contact with the very worst of those who have come out of our gaols is a matter of necessity.

What are the dangers of overcrowding according to the author?

A YOUNG THIEF

John Garwood, General Secretary of the London City Mission, published *The Million Peopled City* in 1853. The book was sub-titled "one half of the People made known to the other half", i.e. the poor to the prosperous. In one chapter he wrote of young offenders:

> Thomas Miller, AGED 8 YEARS, was tried at Clerkenwell at the August sessions, 1845, for stealing boxes, and sentenced to be imprisoned for one calendar month, and once whipped. At the January sessions, 1846, he was again tried . . . for robbing a till . . . . He was subsequently sentenced to seven years transportation, but his sentence was commuted to three months imprisonment.

What aspect of the case particularly concerned the author?

CRIME IN HOXTON

Charles Booth, in *Life and Labour in London* published in the 1880s described Hoxton in North London:

> Hoxton is the leading criminal quarter of London, and indeed of all England . . . . The number of first class burglars is said to be very small . . . . [They] are generally known to the police, and so are the receivers into whose hands they play. Gold or silver stolen anywhere in London comes, it is said, at once to this quarter, and is promptly consigned to the melting pot. Jewellery is broken up; watches are "rechristened". The "fences" or receivers of stolen goods are of all grades, and serve every sort of thief, and in Hoxton, thieves of every kind seem to be represented.

Why was it necessary to melt down gold and silver and break up jewellery?

THE SIXTY ORDERS OF PRIME COVES.

1. Rum-bubbers
2. Coves
3. Groaners
4. Duffers
5. Out-and-outers
6. Coiners
7. Macers
8. Swigs men
9. Bully rocks
10. Lully priggers
11. Ginglers
12. Ken coves
13. Bully huffs
14. Starrers
15. Strollers
16. Mounters
17. Shop-lifters
18. Swadlers
19. Sweeteners
20. Clapper dogens
21. Cloak twitchers
22. Upright men
23. Dubs men
24. Forkers
25. Bullies
26. Autem men
27. Beau nappers
28. Badgers
29. Cadgers
30. Beau traps
31. Twirlers
32. Gammoners
33. Groaners
34. Fencers
35. Spicers
36. High topers
37. Footpads
38. Gamblers
39. Swindlers
40. Shoplifters
41. Sturdy beggars
42. Pad priggers
43. Money lenders
44. Ken crackers
45. Queer culls
46. Rushers
47. Fawney coves
48. Divers
49. Adam iglers
50. Knackers
51. Millers
52. Smashers
53. Filers
54. Gypsies
55. Buffers
56. Priggers
57. Rum padders
58. Gaggers
59. Dragsmen
60. Bloods

Oli compoli, a rogue of the canting crow
On the pot, being in trouble, vex'd
On the mallet, having goods on trust
One two, two blows succeding each other
One, in ten, a parson
Optics, the eyes
Operators, pickpockets
Os chives, bone handle knives
Out and outer, a rum'un, a good fellow at any thing, a trump
Ousted, turned out, thrown
Over the left, it won't do, no go
Over the bender, over the bridge
Overseer, a fellow in the pillory
Owlers, runners and smugglers of wool

P.

Pad, a highwayman who robs on foot
Pad it, to walk
Palm, to fee, to hand over
Pallaird, beggars who borrow children, the better to obtain charity
Panum, victuals
Panum struck, very hungry, wanting something to eat
Pantler, a butler
Param, bread

Parings, clippings of money
Panter, heat
Pat, an accomplice or companion
Patter, slang
Patter slang, to talk flash
Pattered, tried in a court of justice for felony
Pave, the pathway
Pavier's worshop, the street
Peck and boose, victuals and drink
Peel, to strip
Peeper, looking glass
Peepers, eyes
Peel your skin, strip, pull off your clothes
Peery, suspicious
Peg a hack, to drive a hackney coach
Peg, or peg stick, a bender, shilling
Peg tantrums, dead
Penance board, pillory
Persuaders, cudgels or spurs
Peter, a trunk
Peteresses, persons who make it their business to steal boxes from the backs of coaches, chaises, and other carriages
Pewter, money
Pewter, to unload, to drink porter out of a quart pot
Philistines, bailiffs and their crew
Phizog, the face

◁ This list is taken from The Dens of London, published in 1848. Coves are criminals. Can you work out what they did?

CRIMES IN 1841

Of the 2625 offences for which people were tried at the Old Bailey in 1841, over 2000 were for various types of stealing and only three were for murder. Charles Knight, in London: Pictorially Illustrated published in 1843, listed "burglary, coining, forging, horse stealing, housebreaking, letter stealing, receiving stolen goods, sheep stealing and robbery" as being amongst the most common.

THE FORGER

E.A. Carr, in Criminal London published in 1906, described a skilled criminal, working in a back attic in Hoxton:

> Over the coke fire hangs a melting-pot, an iron ladle is lying before it, an electric battery stands on the mantelshelf. On the table, beside a shapeless mass of bright metal, are some odd-looking slabs of plaster of Paris; and seated before it an elderly man in a leather apron at work with his tools, one by one he picks up the glittering white discs that lie before him on a board, nips off from each its long "tail" of metal, and touches up its mulled edge at the point of fracture. … This dingy attic is the workshop of a notorious … "smasher" well known in the old honest days as the cleverest silversmith in Clerkenwell, but an inveterate criminal now.

Of which of the crimes listed by Knight at the Old Bailey was this man guilty?

◁ Slang words used by criminals in London. Many are in Cockney rhyming slang. How many of them are still used today?

Police and Prisons

In 1829 Sir Robert Peel's Metropolitan Police Act became law. Many of the earlier fears that having a uniformed force would lead to a loss of liberty were proved unfounded. The "Bobbies" or "Peelers" were well-disciplined, dressed more like city gentlemen than soldiers and did not carry firearms. By 1840 the whole of London was policed and within twenty years half the English counties had formed their own forces.

POLICE WORK: THE BEAT

Max Schlesinger, in *Saunterings in and out of London* published in 1853, described police work:

> The London policeman knows every nook and corner, every house, man, woman, and child on his beat. He knows their occupations, habits and circumstances. This knowledge he derives from constantly being employed in the same quarter and the same street .... The streets which skirt the banks of the Thames are the most horrible. Here the policeman does not saunter along (as he would elsewhere). Indeed, in many instances they walk by twos and threes ...

Why did the writer feel it to be so important for the policeman to know his local area?

Charles Booth, in *Life and Labour of the People of London* published in several volumes from the late 1880s, praised the police:

> Nearly everyone speaks well of the police, even if some think them not sufficiently a terror to evil-doers .... They do their duty, and take hard knocks and broken heads as all in the day's work ... they may be content merely to frighten boys found playing pitch and toss in some quiet court; ... or [stem] the betting that goes on in all directions.

Why did Booth think that "softly softly" was the most effective approach?

"The Lost Child", a drawing of the 1850s showing the police uniform introduced in 1829 to allay fears of an armed military force.

NIGHT DUTY

Much police work was routine. Buxton Conway, in an article in *Living London* published in 1906, described night duty:

> The night constable's vigil is a lonely one, especially if it is to be passed among the huge, untenanted warehouses of commerical London or the deserted streets of sleeping suburbia, where the silence is not broken by a footfall . . . not even the Officer's own, for he generally dons silent boots for such work, making them himself by affixing strips of rubber tyre to the ordinary footgear.

Would you prefer to do day or night duty? Explain your choice.

PRISON SENTENCES, 1841

On page 34 Charles Knight identified the major crimes. In this extract he lists the sentences at the Old Bailey in 1841:

To death (2 executed)	5
Transportation for life	20
Transportation for 10 or more years	335
Transportation for 7 or more years	387
Imprisonment in Newgate or a House of Correction for 2 years	38
for 18 months	22
for up to 1 year	1784
Other sentences (fines, etc.)	33
Total	**2625**

Find out what transportation was.

Newgate Prison in the 1890s. By this time it was used only for prisoners awaiting trial and for those condemned to death.

PENTONVILLE PRISON

Pentonville was regarded as a model prison when it was opened in 1842. At the start of his sentence the new prisoner was kept in a separate cell and kept apart at all times until he was thought ready to learn a trade and hopefully reformed. Many were then transported to Tasmania, until transportation was ended in 1852. J.C. Platt writing in Charles Knight's *London* in 1843, described the cells in Pentonville:

> Each [cell] is provided with a stone W.C. pan, a metal basin supplied with water, a three legged stool, a small table, a shaded gas burner and a hammock, with mattress and blankets. Each cell is warmed by hot air . . . . None of the prisoners will ever be seen by each other, and in chapel each has his separate box. The Officers wear felted shoes, and can inspect the prisoners, whether in the cell or in the airing yard without being either heard and seen.

What was the major effect of the end of transportation upon the prisons and prisoners?

Leisure and Recreation

What one was able to do depended on one's hours of work, one's pay and whether one had any energy left. Sunday was the only day when the majority could relax, although in the second half of the century many people had Saturday afternoon off. Whilst the public house was the focal point for the working men, both for drinking and meeting friends, drunkenness was a major problem.

THE MUSIC HALL

Walter Greenwood, in *the Wilds of London* published in 1874, described a music hall:

> I might have got in for 3d.; that being the sum charged for admission to the body of the hall, but observing stuck about the walls of the neighbourhood that Ezekial Podgers was to appear for the first time that evening, in addition to the powerful and talented company always to be found at the Grampian, I thought it possible that there might be some little crowding. 6d. admitted me to the gallery, and if I had gone as high as a 1/- I might have taken a seat in the stalls on a form covered with red baize, and smoked a cigar in the distinguished company of Paddy Finnigan, the Chairman ....

Which groups would have been able to afford a 3d. entrance fee?

A theatre poster for the Royal Surrey Theatre. Why ▷ *was the concert held?*

RIDING IN HYDE PARK

George Augustus Sala desribed the scene, in *Twice Round the Clock*, published in 1859:

> Ladies too – real ladies – promenade in an ampitheatre of crinoline difficult to imagine and impossible to describe; some of them with stalwart footmen following them, whose looks beam forth with conscious pride at the superlative toilettes of their distinguished proprietresses .... Little pages, gambolling children .... Can any scene in the world equal Rotten Row at four in the afternoon, and in the full tide of the season?

Why did Hyde Park become such a favourite for the rich?

DERBY DAY

Derby Day at Epsom was one of the major days in the racing calendar. Baedeker's *London and its Environs* of 1885 described its popularity:

> London empties itself annually by road and rail .... The increased facilities of reaching Epsom by train have somewhat dimmed the population of the road, but a decently applied open carriage and pair, holding four persons, will cost £8-10; everything including a hansom cab can be hired for rather less than half that amount. The appearance of Epsom Downs on Derby Day, crowded with myriads of human beings, is one of the most striking and animated sights ever witnessed in the neighbourhood of London, and will interest the ordinary visitor more than the great race itself.

What were the advantages of travelling by train?

LOW LIFE AT THE DERBY

Walter Greenwood, in *The Wilds of London* published in 1874, described the crowds who walked from London:

> They emerged in twos and threes from the road that leads to the metropolis – poor, limping, lame, and ragged ones, wearied nigh to fainting with their long tramp. ... These are the hangers on and pickers up of crumbs that fall from the cloth of gold, the humble servants and willing slaves of the well-to-do. They will bring with them their stock in trade, their boot blackers and shiners, and their humble single brushes with which to "brush you down, sir – for a penny".

By what other means would the poor make money?

RATS! RATS! RATS!

> On Monday, the —, the Canine Fancy may make sure of a treat, by dropping in at Billly Skunto's,
> THE TURNPIT, QUAKER'S ALLEY, SOMERS TOWN
> Rats in the pit at 8.30 precisely.
> Previous to the above entertainment, Mr. Chilley will sing his finch Peel against Edward the Topyobs' celebrated bird for a pound a side.
> Cages uncovered at 8. Plenty of rats for the occasion
> After the sports a harmonious meeting with
> THE RENOWNED BILLY HIMSELF IN THE CHAIR

This is an advertising card distributed in the slums for the illegal "sport" of rat fighting. Can you guess what the two finches had to do (not fight!)

Derby Day at Epsom in the 1890s; not everyone had a seat in the stand.

Markets

SMITHFIELD MARKET

London had many well-established specialist wholesale markets where the shopkeepers and costermongers bought their goods. Old Smithfield is described by Charles Knight in *London: Pictorially Illustrated*, published in 1842:

> The nuisance of holding a market for cattle in the heart of London is not confined to Smithfield. There it is endured for the sake of the profit which it brings to the shops, coffee-houses, inns ... yet a person who resided in Smithfield stated before the Parliamentary Committee that he had lived in Smithfield for 14 years, and found it impossible to sleep in the front of his house on the Sunday night. But the evil extends to all the thoroughfares leading to the market ... there is a danger as well as an inconvenience in driving bullocks and sheep through crowded streets.

Look at a map of London and note the route the drovers would have used. What soon ended the droving trade?

The interior of the Metropolitan Meat Market at Smithfield in the 1880s.

A Billingsgate porter in 1894. What does this market ◁ specialize in?

A STREET MARKET

James Greenwood, in *The Wilds of London* published in 1874, described Hare Street in Bethnal Green:

> The pavement being much too narrow to accommodate the pressing throng, the muddy road was crowded as well. If you wanted chickens, there they were in baskets, in bags, and held up by their legs .... Do you want a goat; there were three "agoin" for the price of dawg's meat .... Were you desirous of possessing a donkey, there was one ...

Why do you think street markets were often more popular than shops?

THE NEW SMITHFIELD

Baedeker's *London and its Environs* of 1885 described the new market:

> Newgate Street, City, is the great meat market in London. The new covered market, opened in 1868, is most admirably fitted up. Subterranean lines connect it with the Metropolitan Railway ....

What advantages did the new market have?

COVENT GARDEN

The British Metropolis, published in 1851, had the following entry:

> The Wholesale dealers and salesmen of fruit, flowers and vegetables, commence their extensive dealings at a very early hour on each market day. The vendors and greeengrocers from all parts of London and its suburbs all congregate soon after 4 o'clock, complete their purchases, with which they drive off, and immediately afterwards the avenues are cleared.

Why was it necessary for the market to start so early?

A SATURDAY EVENING MARKET

Henry Mayhew, in *London Labour and the London Poor* published in 1851, described the scene:

> [Here] the working classes generally purchase their Sunday's dinner; and after pay-time on Saturday night ... the crowd ... is almost impassable .... There are hundreds of stalls, and every stall has one or two lights, either it is illuminated by the intense white light of the new self-generating gas-lamp, or else it is brightened up by the red smoky flame of the old-fashioned grease lamp and one man shows off his yellow haddock with a candle stuck in a bundle of firewood; his neighbour makes a candlestick of a huge turnip, and the tallow gutters over its side ...

Why did people buy on a Saturday night?

Changes in London

During Victoria's reign many changes took place. As the population grew, so London expanded in area and many who could moved away from the central areas.

THE GROWTH OF SOUTH LONDON

Walter Besant, in *South London* published in 1898, described the expansion south of the Thames:

> First, places which had been dotted over with fields and gardens and vacant places such as Southwark and Bermondsey were completely built over and inhabited. [This] first stage was supplemented by the omnibus. Next South London stretched itself out farther; it began to include Camberwell, Brixton, Stockwell, Clapham and Wandsworth. These were separate suburbs ... the inhabitants were ... employers, substantial merchants and flourishing shopkeepers. The clerks lived nearer London .... Lastly came the railway, when London made another step outward .... Then the builder began; he saw that a new class of residents would be attracted by small houses and low rents. The population of south London no longer consists of [the] rich .... Clerks, assistants, and employees of all kind now crowd the morning and evening trains.

Look at a map of London and see the way in which expansion has taken place. Where would the rich have gone?

CHANGES BROUGHT ABOUT BY THE RAILWAY

Not everyone approved of the changes which were taking place. James Wilson, in *The Gazeteer of England and Wales* published in 1876, was very critical of the railway companies:

> The Railway works within the Metropolis have made many amazing changes, and produced many an eyesore. Their viaducts are far from elegant, and form long intersections through the lines of houses; their tubular bridges or iron-girder bridges are ungainly or positively ugly, and spoil or block the vistas of broad streets; and their works, in general, plunge through the capital in all directions ... [they] give many a region a torn and patched appearance ....

Why did Wilson so strongly dislike the changes? Do we view Victorian engineering in the same way?

IMPROVEMENTS – THE COST

One writer who argued that redevelopment took place at the expense of the poor was Lewis Dibden, who wrote an article in *The Quarterly Review* for January 1884:

> In round figures the Metropolitan Board [of Works] cleared away 40 acres of buildings; of these 23 are still, at this moment, vacant, some of the sites have been lying useless and waste for years, with the result that the overcrowding of London is aggravated by some 10,000 people having been squeezed into houses already full to overflowing. The fact is that rebuilding has not kept pace with pulling down.

Why do you think so much land was left vacant?

Temple Bar and the New Law Courts in November 1877 (Illustrated London News, December 1877). Why do you think that Temple Bar was later removed?

CHANGES IN THE CITY

Certainly, the changes were great, as W.J. Loftie described in *London City* published in 1891:

> The changes which London has undergone in the past 20 or 30 years are so great that I can imagine a visitor formerly familiar with the old streets unable to find his way from Temple Bar to the Tower. The very first thing to meet his eyes would be the huge mass of the law courts, where formerly was a rookery .... Then where is Temple Bar? Where is the dingy front of Child's Bank? .... Where, on the opposite side, are the familiar oyster shop and the old Cock [Inn]? All are gone ....

Do you think the writer regrets the changes? Charles Dickens, in an article "Our School" in *Household Words* published on 11 October 1851, wrote:

> We went to look at it, only the last Midsummer, and found that the Railway had cut it up root and branch. A great trunk-line had swallowed the play-ground, sliced away the schoolroom, and pared off the corner of the [school] house ....

Change is continually taking place. How many Victorian buildings remain in your part of London, or where you live? Use a nineteenth-century map to trace what has disappeared.

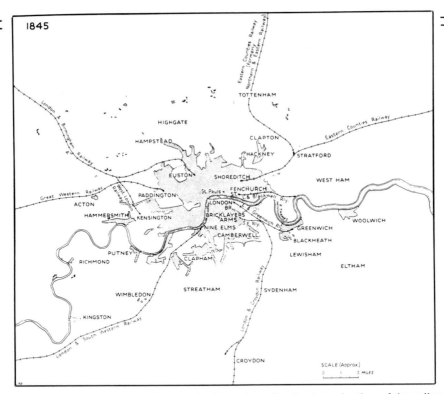

1845

Two maps of London which show the rapid growth of London after the introduction of the railways.

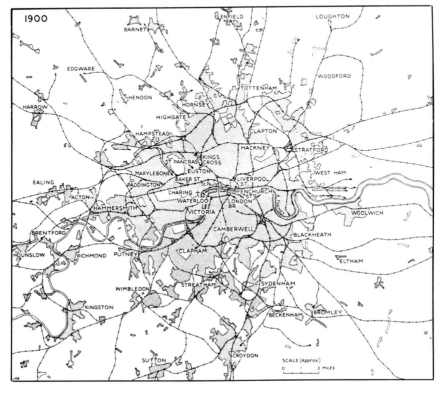

1900

Difficult Words

Board School	a school run by the School Board. The Education Act of 1870 allowed areas to vote for a board and raise an education rate which was levied on property holders towards the cost of running the schools.
breechesmaker	maker of trousers which came just below the knee.
cab	originally a horse-drawn carriage with either two or four wheels (shortened from the French *cabriolet*).
casual labourer	a worker without fixed employment.
census	an official count of population. Britain's first was in 1801 and they have been held every ten years since, except in 1941.
Chartist	one who wanted the vote for all men and other parliamentary reforms. These demands were contained in the Charter, which they presented to Parliament on several occasions in the 1830s and 1840s.
cholera	an infectious and deadly disease which spread from Europe and the East in 1831, 1848-9, 1854 and 1866. At first it was believed that it was spread in the air by smell, but later it was found to be spread in sewage-polluted water.
City of London	strictly, the business area north of London Bridge; roughly equivalent to the area of Roman London.
commuter	one who travels daily to work, usually from a suburb into town or city.
confluent	running together.
coster-monger	a seller of fruit and vegetables from a stall or a barrow.
Crimean War	the war between Russia and Britain and France (1854-6).
distillery	a factory where alcoholic spirits are distilled or made.
dredger	a vessel used for clearing channels.
epidemic	a disease that attacks great numbers of people at a particular time.
equerry	an officer usually in charge of the royal horses.
glazier	a worker who sets glass in window frames.
guinea	a coin originally made from gold from Guinea in Africa; worth 21/- (£1.05).
jappaned	glossy black varnish or lacquer – in the Japanese style.
lodging house	where rooms are rented to lodgers.
mangler	one who works a rolling press (or mangle) for smoothing and drying washing.
Metropolitan Board of Works	established in 1855 to take overall control of the problems of health for London. It took over from the many parishes and water companies. Its first task was the problem of London's sewers.
milliner	one who makes or sells ladies' hats and trimmings.
monopoly	sole power.
omnibus	a large road vehicle carrying many passengers, – the first, in 1829, were horse-drawn.
papier mâché	paper pulped together and varnished to resemble wood.
pauper	one who cannot cope and has to seek help to survive.
plastic arts	shaping in 3D, e.g. sculpture.
quart	a liquid measure equal to two pints.
Rookery	a London slum, e.g. St Giles.
Sessions	the time when a law court is sitting.
stevedore	one who loads and unloads ships.
suburb	an area on the fringe of a city. The majority of its inhabitants travel into the city to work.
Temple Bar	gateway into London. Removed in the nineteenth century to ease traffic.
tenement	usually a building which contains several flats for different families.
transportation	the sending of criminals overseas to serve a prison sentence working in Australia and Tasmania.
workmen's tickets	cheap tickets sold to workers who travelled early in the morning.
yoke	a frame for carrying pails, or joining draught oxen.

Date List

1837 Euston Station opened (London and Birmingham Railway).

1838 Severe frosts in January and February – river frozen; stalls set up on the Thames. Royal Exchange burned down.

1843 Thames Tunnel opened.

1844 New Royal Exchange opened by Queen Victoria and Prince Albert.

1845 City Corporation purchased the Fleet Prison for demolition.

1848 Great Chartist meeting on Kennington Common; 17,000 special constables enrolled, no disorder. Waterloo opened (London and South Western Railway).

1851 Great Exhibition opened.

1852 New Billingsgate Market opened (fish). King's Cross Station opened (Northern and Eastern Railway).

1854 Cannon Street widened. Stock Exchange opened. Paddington Station opened (Great Western Railway).

1855 Metropolitan Board of Works formed. Old Smithfield Market closed.

1856 Street tolls abolished in the City.

1858 Chelsea Bridge opened (freed of tolls 1879). Postal districts established.

1862 Lambeth Bridge and New Westminster Bridge opened. George Peabody gave £150,000 to the London poor – later increased to £½ million.

1863 City police adopted the helmet which replaced the tall hat.

1866 5548 people died of cholera.

1868 Public executions ended.

1869 Blackfriars Bridge, Holborn Viaduct and Albert Embankment opened.

1870 Tower subway opened – ½d. toll for foot-passengers. Victoria Embankment opened.

1871 The Queen opened the Albert Hall.

1872 Guildhall Museum and Library opened.

1873 First Board School opened in Old Castle Street. New Post Office in St Martin-le-Grand. Albert Bridge, Wandsworth and Kew Bridge opened – toll-free.

1874 Chelsea Embankment opened.

1875 Tower of London opened free to the public. New Poultry and Provision Market at Smithfield. New terminus for the Great Eastern Railway at Liverpool Street.

1877 New Billingsgate Fish Market opened.

1881 New Leadenhall Market opened.

1882 New Law Courts (the Old Bailey) opened.

1887 Golden Jubilee celebrations.

1889 London County Council first meet.

1891 Electric Lighting for main streets.

1894 Tower Bridge opened.

1897 Diamond Jubilee celebrations. The Blackwall Tunnel opened.

1899 South Kensington Museum renamed Victoria and Albert Museum.

1901 Death of Queen Victoria.

Money

Always look at what money and wages could buy rather than at what seem low prices to us. It is no use butter being 4p a pound if we only earn 50p a week. Remember that there were 12 old pence (d.) in a shilling (s.) and 20 shillings to the pound. 6d. was the equivalent of 2½p, a shilling (1/-) 5p.

Biographical Notes

BAEDEKER, Karl. German publisher of travel guides. His books always had red covers.

BEAMES, Thomas. A preacher at St James's, Westminster.

BESANT, Walter (1836-1901). Well-known historian and writer about London. His books were very popular and he did much to publicize the problems of the poor, particularly in east and south London.

Book List

BOOTH, Charles (1840-1914). Wealthy ship-owner and social historian. He was particularly concerned with the problems of the poor, old age and the Poor Law. Between 1889 and 1903 the results of his detailed surveys were published in *The Life and Labour of the People of London* (17 volumes).

KNIGHT, Charles (1791-1873). Author and publisher who sought to spread education and informative books to ordinary people. His *London: Pictorially Illustrated* was first published as a part magazine and is found in libraries in either three or six volumes.

MAYHEW, Henry (1812-87). Wrote many articles in the 1840s and '50s. Many of these formed the basis of the large, rambling, but valuable *London Labour and London Poor* (1851).

PEEL, Sir Robert (1788-1850). Home Secretary, 1822-7 and 1827-30. Introduced Metropolitan Police Act 1829. Later Prime Minister, 1835 and 1841-6.

SALA, George Augustus (-1895). Novelist and comic illustrator. His book *Twice Round the Clock* (1859) gives a vivid picture of London in the decade of the Great Exhibition.

SHILLIBEER, George (1797-1866). A Paris coachbuilder. He introduced omnibuses into London in 1829.

SIMON, John (1816-1904). A public health reformer and medical officer. He did much to bring health problems to the public's attention.

SIMS, George (1847-1922). In 1882 he published *How the Poor Live* which reprinted numerous articles he had written for *The Pictorial World*. Throughout the century he publicized the plight of the poor.

TAINE, Hippolyte (1828-93). A French writer who visited England in the 1860s. His *Notes on England* are among the best accounts of English life in the century.

THACKERAY, William Makepeace (1811-63). One of our most famous Victorian novelists.

TILLETT, Ben (1860-1943). Trade Union leader who directed dock strikes of 1889 and 1911. Later became Labour M.P.

WELLS, Herbert George, (1866-1946). Born in Bromley, Kent. Described its development as a suburb in *The New Machiavelli*. He disguised it as Bromstead.

There are very few children's books on Victorian London and so I have listed the books that I found most useful. I have also included a few others which contain excellent illustrations.

Anon (no given author), *The British Metropolis* (1851)

Anon, *London: Pictorially Described* (c.1880)

Baedeker, K., *London and its Environs* (1885)

Beames, T., *The Rookeries of London* (1852)

Booth, C., *Life and Labour of the People of London* (various volumes from the 1880s)

Besant, W., *East London* (1899)

Besant, W., *South London* (1901)

Besant, W., *London in the Nineteenth Century* (1909)

Bradshaw, *Railway Companion* (1840)

Garwood, J., *The Million Peopled City* (1853)

Hughes, M.V., *A London Child of the 1870s* (1934)

Knight, C., *London* (six volumes (1841-3)

Knight, C., *The Cyclopaedia of London* (1851)

Heywood, A., *London* (c.1880s)

Maxwell, H., *Sixty Years a Queen* (1897)

Mayhew, H., *London Labour and the London Poor* (1851)

Murray, J., *London* (1850)

Salmon, J., *Ten Years Growth of the City of London 1881-1891* (1892)

Wilson, J., *Gazeteer of England and Wales* (1876)

RECENT BOOKS

Barker, F. and Jackson, P., *London 2000 Years of a City and its People*, Macmillan (1983)

Betjeman, J., *Victorian & Edwardian London*, B.T. Batsford Ltd (1969)

Burnett, J. (ed.), *Destiny Obscure*, Penguin (1982)

Margetson, S., *Fifty Years of Victorian London*, Macdonald (1969)

Seaman, L.C., *Life in Victorian London*, B.T. Batsford Ltd (1975)

Tames, R., *Victorian London*, B.T. Batsford Ltd (1984)

Weightman, *The Making of Modern London 1815-1914*, Sidgewick & Jackson (1983)

Winter, A., *A Cockney Camera*, Penguin (1975)

Index